T<small>HE LO</small> — whi described a 2009 — has, in fact, been seriously strained by this administration. The White House likes to blame Israeli Prime Minister Benjamin Netanyahu, Washington's longtime whipping boy, for the diplomatic unease that has grown between the two countries. But, in fact, the president, who sanctimoniously forswore "meddling" in the affairs of Iran during the bloody crackdown on protesters against a corrupt election, has had no such compunction about making clear the concessions he expects from Israel or that he regards its intransigent policies as the major obstacle to peace in the Middle East.

Israelis certainly get the picture. In a recent poll, only 4 percent of Israelis said they thought President Obama's policies are supportive of Israel. And many American Jewish leaders, including some strong supporters of Obama, also see the handwriting on the White House wall.

‣ Rep. Howard Berman, the chairman of the House Committee on Foreign Affairs, criticized Obama's call for an end to all growth of "the settlements" and added that Fatah Leader Mahmoud Abbas was now "waiting for the U.S. to present him Israel on a platter."

‣ David Harris, the head of the American Jewish Committee, and Abe Foxman, leader of the Anti-Defamation League – citing the Fatah convention at which Palestinian leaders said they had no intention of renouncing violence, nor in insisting that Hamas abandon its goal of the destruction of Israel – called on Obama to stop ignoring the fact that the key problem in the region was "Arab rejection."

‣ Even Obama's longtime friend and supporter Alan Solow, chairman of the Conference of Presidents of Major American Jewish Organizations, criticized the president's demand that the Israeli presence in

East Jerusalem be strictly circumscribed and that further growth cease.

These leaders were presented with further disturbing evidence of Washington's distancing of Israel when Obama personally attended the ceremony awarding the Presidential Medal of Freedom to Mary Robinson, the former United Nations official who presided over the Durban conference in 2001 that degenerated into an angry hate rally against Israel, America and Jews. And, above and beyond the president's political rhetoric, there were significant changes from the policies of the past several presidencies, notably the reduction of American military support for Israel, including "bunker buster" bombs that could be used in attacks against underground installations, such as Iranian nuclear facilities and terrorist group tunnels into Israeli territory from Lebanon or Egypt, and modern attack helicopters. In April 2009, the United States approved Turkey to provide weapons and military training to the

Lebanese Army, despite Israeli objections (the Lebanese Government has threatened military action against Israel).

Even members of the president's own party have felt constrained to dissociate themselves from Obama's pressure on Israel, especially the pressure to make further territorial concessions to the Palestinians in exchange for "confidence-building" gestures. The number two Democrat in the House of Representatives, Rep. Steny Hoyer, went to great lengths during a visit to Israel in mid-August to draw a line between the president's position and that of Congress. At a press conference, Hoyer had no qualms about pointing out that 368 members of the 435-seat House signed a letter to Obama in May that supported Israel and said that Israel must be free to make its own decisions, and the United States should support those decisions.

The change in the American government's attitude toward Israel is not simply about settlements. Indeed, it's not just about Israel. As President Obama has said, at great length and

> *Obama says he wants to be "fair,"*
> *by which he means that the*
> *Israelis have no special claim*
> *on American sympathies.*

in various settings, he is seeking rapprochement with the entire "Muslim world," and if that doesn't please the Israelis, so be it. He says he wants to be "fair," by which he means that the Israelis have no special claim on American sympathies. He believes that the Palestinians are equally worthy, and he believes, as Arab leaders have long argued, that if Israel will just permit the creation of a Palestinian state, peace will flow like water in this parched part of the world.

Obama has promised to be evenhanded, calling upon both Israel and its enemies to make concessions in the name of peace, as if decades of Israeli concessions and continued Palestinian terrorism, supported by Iran and

Syria, did not count. He's got a set of new scales, and new standards of justice.

As he put it in his celebrated Cairo speech on June 4, 2009:

> *For decades, there has been a stalemate: two peoples with legitimate aspirations, each with a painful history that makes compromise elusive.... [I]f we see this conflict only from one side or the other, then we will be blind to the truth: the only resolution is for the aspirations of both sides to be met through two states, where Israelis and Palestinians each live in peace and security.*
>
> *That is in Israel's interest, Palestine's interest, America's interest, and the world's interest. That is why I intend to personally pursue this outcome with all the patience that the task requires.*

In Obama's view, the theory that Israeli concessions will be matched by its enemies' conversion to peacemaking has not already been tested and failed. Moreover, the idea that the Fatah leadership believes that peace with a secure Israel is "in Palestine's interest" is a pure article of faith. Both the historical record and contemporary evidence strongly suggest the opposite: Palestinian leaders have never accepted the notion that Israel should be secure, and they continue to embrace violence as an acceptable and even admirable method of achieving their ultimate objective, namely, the elimination of Israel altogether.

In the background of this revisionist maneuvering is one looming fact: As he pushes Israel away from the American embrace, Obama has undertaken to make peace with Iran, whose genocidal hatred for America and Israel and bloody war against both requires a very different policy. Sensible Middle East experts understand that there cannot be peace between Israel and the Arabs as long as

---

As he pushes Israel away from the American embrace, Obama has undertaken to make peace with Iran.

Iran exercises a decisive influence over the key terrorist organizations. But Obama has willfully ignored this connection in designing his Mideast plans. In August, Israel was told that the American government would push for tougher sanctions against Iran in exchange for Israeli compliance with Obama's call for the shutdown of settlement expansion – as if the primary need for action against Iran was the role it could play in ending Israeli territorial recalcitrance!

THE VIETNAM MODEL

Obama's efforts to wring new concessions from the Israelis, and the respectful language he uses when discussing Palestinians and Iranians, are reminiscent of the last years of the Vietnam War, when Lyndon Johnson, then Richard Nixon, embraced the vision of a negotiated settlement with the North Vietnamese. The appeals to be evenhanded and the studied use of respectful language about Palestinians and the Iranian regime that we hear today from the president and Secretary of State Hillary Clinton recall similar calls and similar language about our enemies of the 1960s and 1970s. The similarities extend to the other side as well, for the terrorists and their "political arms" use many of the same political and military techniques against Israel today that the North Vietnamese used against us 40 years ago.

This is no accident; Yasser Arafat learned his step-by-step strategy for the conquest of Israel from Ho Chi Minh and his North Vietnamese cadre in 1970. The Palestine Liberation Organization was in crisis, having failed to generate popular support anywhere beyond its limited immediate constituency. In the West, the organization was condemned as terrorist. Arafat knew that he needed to transform his image if the PLO were to gain political traction. He saw that the North Vietnamese and the Viet Cong were fighting effectively against the Americans and were beginning to attract considerable support among their allies. Time would show the wisdom of the North Vietnamese strategy and Arafat's prescience in turning to them for advice.

The Vietnamese strategists (notably General Vo Nguyen Giap and Ho Chi Minh himself) advised the Palestinians to begin to present themselves as a "national liberation movement" and to combine their terrorist attacks with a two-pronged political campaign. In this campaign, they would tone down their uncompromising demand for the destruction of Israel and instead work to achieve this ultimate goal in stages, agreeing to compromise at each stage. In other words, Arafat had to become a "moderate."

While engaging in this cosmetic makeover, the PLO did not – and, according to the available evidence, the leaders of the Palestinian Authority will not –abandon terrorism against Israel. The new face crafted under Hanoi's tutorial simply allowed the terrorists to create a phony distinction between a "moderate" PLO and a "terrorist" group under Abu Nidal, the terrorist gang Arafat pretended to combat but actually created and controlled. Not only did the violence of Abu Nidal enable Arafat to pose as a man of peace by comparison, he was able to secretly deploy the Abu Nidal terrorists to kill off potential rivals within the PLO and other Palestinian groups.

One of Arafat's most successful ploys in his transition to "statesman" was the call for a "two-state solution," an elegant bit of deception that came directly from the North Vietnamese. Neither the North Vietnamese nor the Palestinians saw it as a final solution; in both cases, it was designed to gain territory, which in turn would be used to exert greater pressure on the PLO's enemies.

The stratagem worked extremely well. Ultimately, both Arafat and Le Duc Tho were awarded Nobel Peace Prizes, in tandem with their American and Israeli "negotiating partners." Despite the prestige of the award, peace was not the objective in either case, and the PLO, like Hanoi, continued to wage terror and political war in an effort to decisively shift the balance of power.

The key to that shift in Vietnam was breaking the American will, which was accomplished by a combination of propaganda and military operations. Henry Kissinger paid this effort high tribute when he told Soviet Ambassador Anatoly Dobrynin that the Vietnam War had become a domestic American issue, not just a geopolitical matter. Over time, the North Vietnamese drained the willingness of the American public to maintain support for their South Vietnamese ally.

As American public opinion shifted, the North Vietnamese were smart enough to permit the Americans to save face. Instead of demanding a humiliating surrender, they signed agreements with the Nixon administration, purporting to respect the integrity of South Vietnam. In reality, they had no intention of respecting the agreements; indeed, shortly thereafter, the United States abandoned its support for South Vietnam, and the North's armies moved in.

The Palestinians are still far away from such a moment of triumph, but they have made progress of a sort unthinkable, say, in 1970. Their greatest victory is political: They have convinced much of the world that Israel is Goliath and they are little David; that their ambitions extend no further than statehood; and that simple fairness demands that the two sides be treated in the same manner. The Palestinians have been so successful that the doctrine of the "two-state solution" is now universally accepted, above all, by the key actors: the American and Israeli governments and people, and even terrorist leaders who openly embrace terrorism against civilians, yet are now described as "militants" or even "moderates." But there is no more reason to accept this view of Israel's enemies today than there was to believe that the North Vietnamese were really moderates in the 1970s.

Israel's enemies happily admit that their political strategy is based on the deception of Israel and the United States. Mohammed Dahlan, Fatah's leader in Gaza, openly admitted that Yasser Arafat misled the world when he made a show of denouncing Palestinian terrorism: "Arafat would condemn [terrorist] operations by day while at night he would do honorable things." By "honorable things," of course, Dahlan was referring to these acts of terrorism themselves.

Similarly, Fatah leader Abbas has condemned "all forms of terrorism," but he is quick to add that the "legitimate struggle" should not be called terrorism and should not be stigmatized. Abbas candidly told a Jordanian newspaper last year that, whenever the Palestinian Authority suspended its terror attacks, it was not because it was renouncing violence but because it was tactically or materially unable to act as it wished. "Now we are against armed conflict because we are unable," he said, adding wistfully, "In the future stages, things may be different." After all, he added, "we taught everyone what resistance is, including the Hezbollah, who were trained in our camps." As if to underline Abbas's words, at the recent Palestinian Authority Congress, when the presence of two well-known terrorists was announced, there was spontaneous applause.

The Palestinians are so grateful to the North Vietnamese, and with such good reason, that the writings of General Giap were translated into Arabic by Fatah and hold an appropriate place of honor alongside the doctrines of Che Guevara and Mao Zedong.

Nor have Israel's enemies forgotten the North Vietnamese's bottom line: The political strategy and the use of terrorism are the preliminaries to the final confrontation. General Giap conducted a terror war against the South, the Americans and other allies at the same time that he was creating a full-fledged army ready someday to roll into his opponent's capital city. The same is true today, as Hamas and Hezbollah fire missiles and rockets into Israel, preparing for the ultimate conquest.

If it is easy to understand the Palestinians' adoption of the techniques of North Vietnamese political warfare, it is more difficult to explain why Obama would give the

Palestinians the same opportunity that Nixon gave the Vietnamese, especially since he has none of the excuses that Nixon had. In Nixon's day, Americans were fighting and dying in the war in Vietnam; no American soldier is at risk defending Israel. In the 1970s, there was a vast popular movement in the United States that supported retreat from Vietnam, and there was very little support for the continued defense of the South. Nothing of the sort exists today. On the contrary, popular support for Israel is very strong in America. American policy does not try to prop up a feckless regime in Tel Aviv unable to defend itself, but adamantly (in the case of Iran) restrains Israel from taking the battle to its enemies, who are also America's own.

Subtly shifting American policy toward Israel is not a matter of political calculation by President Obama, but rather an expression of his own convictions. We are entitled to ask if he has a sound basis for those convictions. To date, the answer must be that, despite his impressive academic background, the president often has shown ignorance of the central elements of the Middle East, from the content of Islamic and Jewish doctrines to the basis for the Jewish claim to the land of Israel, and the role of violence in world history.

THE MUSLIM WORLD ACCORDING TO OBAMA

In his celebrated speech in Cairo in June, the President called for peace in the Middle East. In an effort to appeal to the best traditions of the three monotheistic religions that came from the region, he read quotations from their holy books:

> *The Holy Koran tells us, "O mankind! We have created you male and a female; and we have made you into nations and tribes so that you may know one another."*

> *The Talmud tells us: "The whole of the Torah is for the purpose of promoting peace."*

> *The Holy Bible tells us, "Blessed are the peace-makers, for they shall be called sons of God."*

The people of the world can live together in peace. We know that is God's vision. Now, that must be our work here on Earth.

Few commented on these quotations at the time, but anyone reading them today must be struck by what distinguishes the Koran from the others: the lack of the word "peace." "Know one another" is certainly not the same thing as "promoting peace," and dividing the world into tribes and nations and men and women is very different from calling for an end to conflict. Yet Obama presented the three quotations as if he thought that they were somehow equivalent.

Indeed, it is very hard to cite the Koran, even selectively, for evidence that Islam, like Judaism and Christianity, yearns for peace. In the run-up to the Yitzhak Rabin–Yasser Arafat handshake on the White House lawn in 1993, President Clinton's speechwriters called on the great American scholar of Islam, Bernard Lewis, for a quotation from the Koran that the president could use for the occasion. Lewis cited one from memory. "Not that one," he was told. "We've already used that one. We need another one." Lewis was forced to reply, "I don't think there is another one."

Obama's Cairo speech was also full of misstatements about the history of the Muslim world, all designed to demonstrate that Islam made many important contributions to Western civilization. There are such contributions, but many of the examples the president used were, at best, misleading, above all his contention that "Islam has a proud tradition of tolerance." In fact, there is not a single instance in the long history of Islam in which Jews have been "tolerated" (at least as we use the word today) by a Muslim ruler or government. In every case, the Jews have been stigmatized as formally inferior, forced to identify themselves as such (sometimes having to wear certain clothing or symbols), and compelled to pay onerous financial tribute to their rulers. No wonder that, in the mid-20th century, the Jews of the Middle East fled their ancient homelands for freedom in what would become

Israel, a journey toward freedom made all the more dramatic by the fact that Muslim Arabs now live, work and even serve in Parliament in this Israel, alongside Christians and Jews.

Obama's refusal to recognize the historical or religious differences between Islamic and Judeo-Christian attitudes toward peace suggests that, despite his years in Muslim Indonesia, he knows very little about Islam. The Koran is chock-full of calls to dominate and slaughter infidels, with particular emphasis on the Jews. Its intimations of genocide have been codified into an action plan by our major enemy (and Israel's) in the Middle East today – Iran. The Ayatollah Ruhollah Khomeini, who created the Islamic Republic of Iran in the late 1970s, left a time capsule 30 years ago that President Obama has unfortunately not yet opened:

Those who know nothing of Islam pretend that Islam counsels against war. Those are witless. Islam says 'Kill the unbelievers. . . . Kill them, put them to the sword and scatter their armies!'. . .

There are thousands of other [Koranic] *verses and hadiths urging Muslims to value war.... Does all that mean that Islam is a religion that prevents men from waging war? I spit upon those foolish souls who make such a claim.*

The Islamic Republic's Supreme Leader Ali Khamenei proclaims himself the spiritual guide for all Muslims. This is not mere cant. As we have learned at great cost in both Iraq and Afghanistan, the Iranians have funded, armed, protected and guided Islamist terrorists of different cults and nationalities and directed their murderous fervor toward us and our allies for more than three decades. The Iranian regime routinely organizes large crowds to chant "Death to America!" and "Death to Israel!" Its agents and military officers carry out those threats throughout the Middle East and even in cities as remote from this region as Buenos Aires, Argentina, where the Israeli Embassy and later a Jewish social center were bombed by Iranian-sponsored terrorists. All in the name of a version of Islam that boasts tens of millions of followers and openly states that evocations of peace are a sham.

Nonviolence

President Obama's ignorance of Muslim history and theology is not only unbecoming for a world leader but also very dangerous for a man facing a global explosion of radical Islamic violence, much of it aimed against the United States itself. His ignorance of such fundamental matters goes hand-in-hand with a collection of politically soothing beliefs about human and political nature that is also based upon historical distortions. The most important of these is the happy thought that serious problems cannot be resolved by violence and that America's own history "proves" that. In Cairo, Obama put it this way:

Resistance through violence and killing is wrong and does not succeed. For centuries, black people in America suffered the lash of the whip as slaves and the humiliation of segregation. But it was not violence that won full and equal rights. It was a peaceful and determined insistence upon the ideals at the center of America's founding.

Except that it certainly wasn't. The bloodiest war of the 19th-century world – the American Civil War – was the most important event in the elimination of slavery in this country, without which Dr. Martin Luther King's non-violent campaign against segregation would have been unimaginable. For that matter, "America's founding" was itself the result of violent war, and George Washington, the victorious commanding general in that conflict, became our first president.

President Obama is predictably a great admirer of committed anti-Israel activists such as Mary Robinson and Obama's like-minded friend, Prof. Rashid Khalidi, whose view of America's proper role in the Middle East was summarized by Martin Kramer:

> [T]*here is no cause that could ever justify an American use of force in the Middle East.... It is America's use of strong armed force – and the parallel violence of Israel – which have provoked*

[23]

the counter-violence of the extremists. If America were to give up its bullying ways, and address the "grievances" of Arabs and Muslims, the latter would regain their respect for America. There are no pathologies in the Middle East that haven't been caused by imperialism, and no pathologies that can't be cured by displays of American humility and penitence.

There is very little, if anything, in those words with which President Obama is known to differ. If anything, his repeated apologies for presumed American sins in the past, including the use of armed force, suggest that he fully believes them. His calls for "engagement" and his rote insistence that the fractious conflicts of the Middle East can be resolved by addressing grievances at the negotiating table go hand-in-hand with those beliefs.

* * *

As usual, American Jews overwhelmingly supported the Democratic candidate for president in November 2008, and some of the president's most important advisers are Jewish. Until quite recently, most American Jews thought of Obama as their friend. Yet, just as he has revealed surprising ignorance of the Koran, he recently demonstrated unfamiliarity with some basic Jewish beliefs, above all, the relationship between man and the Almighty.

On August 19, President Obama held a conference call with 1,000 rabbis, trying to enlist their support for his health-care program. Although the Jewish high holidays were a full month away, he wished them all a happy new year and reminded them that during the "days of awe," the Lord decides the destiny of every human being for the forthcoming year. Jews pray that they be inscribed in the Book of Life, and that they be granted good health. Obama referred to those prayers and added,

"We are God's partners in matters of life and death."

No observant Jew would accept that statement. As the writer Andrew Klavan wittily observed, "When God tells Jeremiah (1:5), 'Before I formed you in the womb, I knew you,' or when he sarcastically asks Job (38:17), 'Have the gates of death been opened unto thee? Or hast thou seen the doors of the shadow of death?' does that sound to you like a guy discussing matters with his partners?" In these matters, Jews are supplicants, not partners.

Nor is Obama well-informed about the nature of Zionism, the basis of the Jews' claim

---

It is hard to negotiate successfully if you don't understand the most fundamental convictions of the parties you insist on bringing to the table.

---

to the land of Israel. He said in Cairo that Israel's right to exist derives from the terrible oppression of Jews throughout the centuries, especially the Holocaust. But Theodor Herzl, the father of Zionism, and all of the other founders of the country never said any such thing. They insisted that the Jewish presence on that land has been continuous for thousands of years and that modern Israel is simply the restoration of a Jewish state that was promised to Abraham, entrusted to Moses, conquered by Joshua and ruled by David, Solomon and their successors.

It is hard to negotiate successfully if you don't understand the most fundamental convictions of the parties you insist on bringing to the table.

IRAN

Barack Obama has long promised to offer talks to Iran with no preconditions, and he and almost all of the pundits in the American media have claimed that this is a radical departure from past American practice. But, in fact, every American president from Jimmy Carter to George W. Bush has negotiated with the Iranians, with an obvious lack of any meaningful result. One of Bill Clinton's top Iran experts, Ken Pollack, sadly commented that the United States had tried almost everything to improve relations. We had brandished every stick and dangled every carrot, but the Iranians were not interested. They do not want a grand bargain with the United States. What do they want?

When James Bond, lying on a gold sheet as a laser beam sliced through toward his most sensitive body parts, asked Goldfinger, "Do you expect me to talk?" Goldfinger shook his head. "No, Mr. Bond, I expect you to die." That is the Iranian policy toward the United States and Israel: death. The Iranian tyrants do not make a substantive distinction between us and the Israelis; it is only a difference in size between the Great Satan and the Little Satan. Both are malevolent and must be destroyed. When Iranian leaders speak of removing Israel from the map, they should be taken seriously, and that is why Israeli leaders are right to describe Iran as an *existential* threat. They know that Iran is training, arming and funding Israel's enemies, primarily Hamas, Hezbollah, Fatah and Islamic Jihad. They know that Arafat was the first honored guest of the Islamic Republic in 1979 and that Hezbollah is an Iranian proxy. And they know, as every honest analyst does, that Iran is building atomic bombs.

In like manner, Iran is a serious threat to the United States. Prior to 9/11, Iranian-sponsored terrorists were the leading killers of Americans, as befits a regime repeatedly branded by the State Department as the world's leading backer of terrorism. During our war in Iraq, and now again in Afghanistan, the greatest cause of American casualties has been the infernal explosive devices more often than not provided to our enemies by the Iranian Revolutionary Guards. Iran's actions against us are not limited to overseas battlefields, for our law-enforcement organizations have abundant evidence of Iranian-backed sleeper cells inside the United States. Every so often, Iranian personnel from their United Nations offices are expelled, having been found photographing bridges, tunnels and subway stations in and around New York City. These are not tourist shots to amuse their families after Sunday dinner.

In short, both Israel and the United States have every reason to challenge the Iranian regime, nukes or no nukes. Iran would be a mortal threat to Israel and the United States, even if there were no nuclear weapons program. The mullahs' drive for atomic bombs makes the threat a matter of life and death. There are several ways to lessen, or even negate, this nuclear threat, ranging from military action against the facilities where the uranium is being enriched and bombs constructed to successfully promoting regime change in Tehran. One can imagine a successful outcome to such actions against Iran if the United States and Israel worked together, but the task is daunting indeed if it is left to Israel alone. That is why the Israelis have worked so hard over the years to convince American leaders to adopt an effective Iran policy.

Like its predecessor, the Obama administration has refused to join the Israelis in planning a joint military operation against Iran, and while American officials talk a great deal about bringing harsh sanctions against Tehran, thus far there is no reason to believe that countries like China and Russia will permit the United Nations Security Council to enforce effective measures. Meanwhile, Israelis and Americans are targeted ever more closely by Iranian proxy forces.

President Obama apparently believes that if progress is made toward resolving the Palestinian issue, he will be able to enlist the Arab countries in an effective diplomatic campaign to moderate Iran's behavior. But he has the causal relationship backwards. Iran drives the terror war against Israel, and therefore, the Palestinian question cannot be resolved until

Iran has been dealt with. In all likelihood, peace will not be granted to Israel as long as the current regime is in power in Tehran.

The key to Middle East peace is not in Israeli or Palestinian hands, but in the bloody grasp of the Iranian regime. And, as the words of the Ayatollah Khomeini make clear, the Islamic Republic of Iran firmly believes that its war against America and Israel is divinely sanctioned. That belief is unlikely to be shaken by an offer of good-faith negotiations from President Obama. Anyone who thinks that the ayatollahs are likely to be swayed by reason need only remember what happened when Iranian democrats protested a rigged election. The savagery visited upon them gives a pale preview of what the Islamic Republic has in mind for Israelis and Americans.

It is difficult for Obama to accept these harsh facts because he is intellectually and emotionally committed to a very different view of the world. Arguments alone are unlikely to change his mind; as a result, facts on the ground may provide his education. If, as many Iranian leaders have promised, a devastating attack is directed against the United States or Israel, or against American troops in the Middle East or elsewhere, Obama might reconsider his worldview. Or, less catastrophically, Tehran's continued insults and scorn for his silky words might also compel him to look for other strategies.

In either case, Americans and our Israeli friends will have paid a very high price for his failure to recognize the true nature of the Middle East conflict and to have dealt with it seriously and effectively. The only saving grace of America's current muddied policies is that while Barack Obama might be terribly confused about the basic facts and naive in his faith in the basic peacefulness of the Palestin-

The key to Middle East peace is not in Israeli or Palestinian hands, but in the bloody grasp of the Iranian regime.

ian terrorist elites and their Iranian masters, the Israelis know they must either prevail or die. And this, to paraphrase Samuel Johnson, has concentrated their minds wonderfully.

First American edition published in 2009 by Encounter Books, an activity of Encounter for Culture and Education, Inc., a nonprofit, tax exempt corporation. Encounter Books website address: *www.encounterbooks.com*

Manufactured in the United States and printed on acid-free paper. The paper used in this publication meets the minimum requirements of ANSI/NISO z39.48–1992 (R 1997) (*Permanence of Paper*).

FIRST AMERICAN EDITION

LIBRARY OF CONGRESS CATALOGING-IN-PUBLICATION DATA

Ledeen, Michael Arthur, 1941–
Obama's betrayal of Israel / by Michael A. Ledeen.
p.   cm. — (Encounter broadsides)
ISBN-13: 978-1-59403-462-6 (pbk. : alk. paper)
ISBN-10: 1-59403-462-1 (pbk. : alk. paper)
1. United States—Foreign relations—Israel. 2. Israel—Foreign relations—United States. 3. Obama, Barack. 4. United States—Foreign relations—2009– I. Title.
E183.8.I7L43   2009
327.730569409´05—dc22
2009036819

10 9 8 7 6 5 4 3 2 1